Fat Naked Poetry

Jim Larsen

Copyright © 2015 Jim Larsen
All rights reserved.
ISBN-978-0-9912920-4-2

This book dedicated to any and all that get what life is all about and can see the humor in just about any situation.

Fat Naked Man Doing Tai Chi on the Beach

Fat Naked Man doing Tai Chi on the beach,
must you stand so close?

Sunshine
Blue sky
Waves so majestic
Beautiful beautiful day.
My heart doth expand,
My spirit doth soar.
Fat naked man,
from where did you appear?

Fat naked man doing Tai Chi on the beach,
you are a thief!
A thief of sight!
A thief of vision!
What did you do with my ocean?
Where did you take my sea?

Fat naked man, must you squat so?
Fat naked man- the crack of your ass holds no appeal to me!
There are five things I had hoped would never be seen by these, my eyes.
Thank you, Fat Naked Man,
Now I have seen four.

Fat naked man, stay out of the honky tonks,
Your Tai Chi has no power here.
Stay on your beach.
Stay in your world.
Fat Naked Man doing Tai Chi on the beach
Must you stand so close?

Jim Larsen

Bacon in the Pig Slop

Bacon in the pig slop!
Bacon in the pig slop!

I am a little piggy,
I'll eat anything you give me
pasta, swai, ahi too,
but there's only one thing I ask from you.
Put more
Bacon in the pig slop!
Bacon in the pig slop!

It may seem wrong
but it tastes so right.
I'd love to eat bacon
every single night.
So if you do this for me
you'll see this little piggy dance with glee.
Put more
Bacon in the pig slop!
Bacon in the pig slop!

And just to put your mind at ease
there's no such thing as "Mad Pig Disease"
so if you could
and if you please
give us more ham and cheese
more pork chops
ham hocks
and pork belly stew
with one more thing
and I'll love you.
More bacon in the pig slop!
Bacon in the pig slop!

More! More! More! Please don't stop!
I want to eat bacon until I pop!

You may think it's wrong

to feed us our own kind.
That's your own moral projection,
we don't mind!
We love
Bacon in the pig slop!
Bacon in the pig slop!

Tomato! Tofu! And Gorilla Munch
are the things I love a bunch.
But there's something that I like more,
it's what I have a craving more.
It's something simple you could be making.
You know what it is, so let's get shaking!
Get in the kitchen and gab a pan
light up the stove
turn on the fan.
Maybe a little grease will splatter,
just wipe it up
it don't matter.
Have some for you
but save some for me.
Porcine cannibalism
does not spell indecency.
So don't forget
try to remember
more
Bacon in the pig slop!
Bacon in the pig slop!

BACON! BACON! BACON! BACON! BACON! BACON! BACON!
BACON! BACON! BACON! BACON!
Bacon in the pig slop!

Don't stop.

Butter Tea

Butter Tea, Butter Tea
Every morning, Butter Tea.
Some for you, some for me.
Fill up my cup.
I'll drink it up.
Butter Tea, Butter Tea.

Excuse me,
I have to pee.
I drank too much
Butter Tea, Butter Tea.

What's in it?
I'm not sure.
Butter yes,
but I know there's more to
Butter Tea, Butter Tea.

Do you see the Butter Tea?
We drink it hot,
but not spicy.
I work here
so I get it free.
I sure love my Butter Tea.

I will bet
it's the greatest thing about Tibet
and you'd agree
if you drink with me
a delicious cup of Butter Tea.
Butter Tea-hee-hee-hee,
I'm all giddy for Butter Tea.

On the ground or in a tree,
I gotta have my Butter Tea,
Butter Tea. Butter Tea, Butter Tea.
La la la la la

la la la la lee
I sold my soul for Butter Tea.
Butter Tea!

Jim Larsen

Moon Over Sara

Hide hide hide
Sara can not hide
Sara can not hide from the moon.

So many stars
Billions and billions in the entire galaxy
But only one moon. Sara's moon
Sara Sara's moon.

The Moon of Sara's womanhood.
Sara's moon.
Sara Sara's moon.
Sara cycles with the moon.

Sara's cycles
Moon cycles.
When the moon is full
So are Sara's ovaries.
See Sara's ovaries
Cycle with the moon.

Hey diddle diddle
The cat and the fiddle
The dish ran away
With the lining of Sara's uterus
To the Dark Side of the Moon.
The cow jumped over Sara's ovaries.

Moon over Sara
Sara over the moon.
When the moon is a crescent in the sky
So are Sara's ovaries.

The cat's in the cradle
with a silver spoon
Little boy blue
And the man in Sara's womb.

Sometimes you might look up and see the moon in the middle of the day, and you might also look up and see Sara in the middle of the day too.

Moon moon moon
Sara cycles with the moon.
She lives on the mauka end of the rainbow.
Rainbow.
Rainbow Bright.
Light Bright
Silly Putty.
Lincoln Logs.
Toys from Sara's childhood
Left behind to cycle with the moon.

Jim Larsen

Little Weed

Hello little plant growing in the garden.
Do you really think you belong?
Look at yourself
do you see what is wrong?
You're not pretty like the other plants
and so you have to die.

We have a word for you, ugly little plant growing in the garden.
We call you a "weed."
You didn't come from our seed.
You're just here to feed
from the sun
from the light
from the air
from the rain
that is meant for the other plants,
the pretty plants growing in the garden.

I'll pull you from your roots,
vile little weed growing in the garden.
Don't you see the others? The others in the pile?
Tossed there with a smile? It took them a while
to die.
Yanked from their roots from the garden.

Take warning
take heed
grotesque little weed
growing in the garden.
You're not welcome here,
so live in fear
Fear! If you dare enter the garden
for the garden is for the pretty plants.
Only pretty plants are welcome in our garden.

Mauka Billy

Get your work clothes on
there's work to be done
no time for fun
dancing is for girls
why you wearing that dress for anyway,
Mauka Billy?

Hey hey Mauka Billy,
don't you know nothing?
You gotta push the clutch in
if you gonna change gears.
Ain't you never driven a tractor before?

Give him a shovel.
Maybe he can at least dig potatoes.
Damn your stupid,
Mauka Billy.

Hey hey Mauka Billy
where'd you get that baby at?
Don't hold him by his feet.
He don't want to suckle at your teat.
You know better than to touch him there.
His momma's probably worried. You should give him back,
Mauka Billy.

Good Lord,
Mauka Billy
Why you wearing mascara?
Mr. Reinier ain't gonna wait forever.
He needs you in the coal mine.
Ain't we talked about them pointy shoes?
Come on now,
Mauka Billy.

Born in a boxcar
Third of June nineteen forty two.

Jim Larsen

Never saw the light.
Never won a fight.
Not really a boy
Not quite a girl
Wears them shorts that fit too tight.

Got a sip of water for his fourth birthday.
Ain't got no name except for Mauka Billy.
Little black child,
Mauka Billy.
First words out of his mouth,
"What's wrong with me?"
Little sad child
Mauka Billy.

Born to dance
Never got the chance.
Be careful crossing the street,
cars don't slow down for your kind,
not around here,
Mauka Billy.

Hey Mauka Billy,
Why you talk so funny?
Why your nose always runny?
Why don't you shut your pie hole,
Mauka Billy?

Mauka Billy.
Blessed child
Mauka Billy.
You're better than this.
I know you know this.
You've glimpsed the light,
Haven't you
Mauka Billy?

I know a place
a far away place.
They will accept you there for your grace.

Get out of the coal mine
Mauka Billy.

Just get on the train
you got your ticket in your hand.
I'll pick you up at the station
Mauka Billy.

Around here
Nobody cares about the color of your skin
or what you put your genitals in.
People will pay to watch you dance
Mauka Billy.

Mauka Billy!
Mauka Billy!
Mauka Billy!
Do you hear the crowd?
They're chanting your name all out loud.
They're here to see you dance!
Dance, Mauka Billy! Dance!
Your dream has come true at last
Mauka Billy!

You are a star!
You've come so very very far!
You'll never shovel coal again.
You don't have to pretend
to be something you're not
just to defend
the person you are,
Mauka Billy!

Hey, what you watching that stupid stuff on TV for? Change the damn channel! Sherry Lewis and Lambchop's gonna be on Ed Sullivan tonight. Change the damn channel, I said! Do it now before I punch you in the face!
Punch you in the face!
Punch you in the face!
Do it now before I...

Jim Larsen

Hey...what the hell is this?
Ain't that Mauka Billy?
Dressed up all dumb and silly?
What's he doing on TV?
Damn, that really is Mauka Billy.

Hey did you see?
Mauka Billy was on TV
dancing for the world to see.
Didn't we used to throw eggs at him?

Yep.
That was Mauka Billy
Wearing them shorts all tight and frilly.
How did he get so high faulting?
Does he think he's better than us?
Let's teach him a lesson.
We're gonna get you,
Mauka Billy.

Let's get out of here,
Mauka Billy.
I have a bad feeling.
Forboding and doom have engulfed me.
Let's get out of here, come on, let's go.
Please Mauka Billy!
Please!

Oh, Juan Enrico,
You know I don't like your superstitious mumbo jumbo...

Look out Mauka Billy!
He has a gun!
Don't shoot! Don't shoot!
Mauka Billy!
Look out!

Bang!

A small mind with a big gun.

Mauka Billy nearly lost his life,
Nearly widowed his same-sex wife.
But thank God
Thank God
Thank God
His aim was bad
because that would have been way too sad
if the world had lost you that day
that way
Mauka Billy.

So, Mauka Billy didn't die that day, but the noise from the gun caused permanent damage to his left ear and he had problems with being dizzy sometimes because of it, and that kind of messed up his dancing a little bit. But he didn't give up and he eventually overcame and resumed his dance career, becaming more popular than ever, especially after 60 Minutes did that thing about him. He's still alive today. He and Juan Enrico live in upstate Vermont, retired to a simple life. He doesn't dance anymore, arthritis to his hips and knees finally forced him into retirement, but he has no regrets. There's been some talk that Eddie Murphy might produce a movie about his life, but it doesn't look like it's really going to happen. And that's the true story of Mauka Billy. Oh, and I should tell you this. Never again did Mauka Billy ever set foot in a coal mine.

Jim Larsen

Yellow Dog

Mornings at First Cup Cafe
I drink my coffee
My breakfast tastes good.
My morning routine in India.
At my feet, there sleeps a yellow dog
tired from a night of barking.

Across the street, a nunnery.
Above the nunnery, trees.
Monkeys in the trees
you have captivated the yellow dog.

Monkeys over the nunnery
I too, am captivated.
That you exists, perhaps is what fascinates me.
Where else have I been where I can be entertained by monkeys in
trees over a nunnery?
Been entertained by a yellow dog whose interest is as mine?

Monkeys in the trees over the nunnery
You have united the yellow dog and me.
What else do we have in common?
I would just be a traveler enjoying my coffee
and he a lazy dog relaxing.

You have bonded us in a point of interest like no other species
could do,
would do,
or want to do.

Monkeys over the trees in the nunnery
keep on doing what you do.
Keep on fascinating travelers to this land
with the yellow dog.

How many before me?
How many still to arrive?

Why?

Why is everyone afraid of gluten?
Gluten is what I love.
Gluten is a gift from the Heavens
Carried on the wings of a dove.

These people who don't like gluten
I wish I could give them a shove...
Off a cliff.
And as they plunge to their death, in the last microsecond of their life, maybe they'll have an awakening and ask themselves,

Why was I afraid of gluten?
Was it ever really that bad?
Why didn't I embrace gluten?
Was my life really so pointless and sad?

If I had my life to live over again,
I would for my own sake
Put gluten in my waffles,
My cookies and cake.

I wouldn't be afraid of gluten.
I would lead the charge and say,
"Hip-hip-hooray for gluten!
It makes me so happy and gay!"

I think the world is changing;
People are abandoning fear.
With more and more people loving gluten
A revolution is certainly near.
Soon we will all eat gluten
And the world will be as one.
Then if they would get over this vegan craze,
My work here on Earth will be done.

When I die, I'll stand at the Pearly Gates
And Saint Peter will say to me,
"I'm so glad you loved gluten

And didn't reject it needlessly.
Nobody ever gets sick from gluten;
There's no such thing as an allergy.
It's just something somebody made up.
Then it caught on.

Then 'gluten free' became a thing and these companies started catering to it, and it's been going on for years. But now you're dead and gluten had nothing to do with it, it's because a coconut fell on your head. Gluten, while you were alive actually gave you super powers. That's why you could fly and see through walls, but that's all over now because you're here, so come on into Heaven and have a ham sandwich and a Pepsi if you like, and Mary Magdalen will give you a foot massage. You can tell the living,

There's nothing wrong with gluten.
Gluten is your friend.
So just keep on eating gluten.
Eat it until the end."

Luke Duke, Suddenly Poetic

With a beat of the heart
nothing can stay.

Two cousins in the belly of the Dixie bullet
fleeing from unjust, unrest
suspended, hanging, flung through the air-
a Phoenix bursting forth from the Georgia clay.

With a beat of the heart, nothing can change.
Except everything.

The clouds above, nonconforming
never saying "I am content"
for longer than a thrice blinked eye.

If with the next beat of my heart
I should become that cloud,
if The General Lee should fly
too high
too fast
too sudden

If he should come down too hard
into the shine-infested Georgia mud
if the mountain should get me
the way the law never could,
those who carry on,
let them say:
"He was a good old boy. He never meant no harm."

Papayas

I worked in the kitchen with Yoshiko. Yoshiko explained how to prepare papayas. She told me to handle the papayas as you would handle a lady. This says a lot to me about how Japanese men treat their women-folk, and to be honest, this scares me more than I have as yet let onto.

So, according to Yoshiko, if I were Japanese, this is how I would be expected to treat my woman: first, I would wash her off with cold water, because you never know, rats may have been crawling on her over night. Secondly, I would want to chop her head and her butt off and slice her in half length wise.

After that, I would want to scoop all the inside gunk out with a spoon without digging too much into the meaty part. And if I am really lucky, I'll be able to get the spoon underneath that thin membrane and get all the gunk out with one scoop.

And finally, I would quarter the sections and put them into a serving bowl, but I would want to do it nicely because, presentation is everything. And that, according to Yoshiko, is how Japanese men treat their women.

Santa Put Rudolph Down

Rudolph the reindeer done broke his leg
So Santa put him down.
It's the saddest thing you ever saw
It happened in our town.

Santa Claus loved that reindeer so
He raised him from a fawn.
Now his shiny red nose won't glow no more
but his memory will live on.

Rudolph the reindeer had broke the reins
And came down a little too hard.
He fractured his leg and went into shock
Then collapsed in my back yard.

All the other reindeer gathered around
And remembered when they used to pick on him
they all started to cry and felt real bad
as his poor nose started to dim.

Santa Claus knew what he had to do
for the sake of humanity
He couldn't let him suffer so he aimed his gun
And put Rudolph down in history.

Rudolph the reindeer done broke his leg
So Santa put him down
It's the saddest thing you ever saw
It happened in our town.

Santa Claus is feeling such grief
He has to cancel Christmas this year.
So if he didn't get to your house
don't you shed a tear.

Other people have problems bigger than you
So show some sympathy

Jim Larsen

Send a little love to Santa Claus
As you trim your Christmas tree.

Rudolph the reindeer done broke his leg
So Santa had to put him down
It's the saddest thing he ever had to do
It happened in our town.
It happened in our town.

Gentleman

One time I tried to be a gentleman and open a door for a lady, but it was a revolving door. It got real messy real fast.

Raven's Craving

Raven has a cravin'
She wants an omelet real bad.
So we found a place that serves them.
A waffle is what I had.
Raven has a cravin'
She wants an omelet real bad.

The restaurant we went to
had a picture of Willie Nelson on the wall.
Willie Nelson played Uncle Jessie in The Dukes of Hazard movie.
He isn't very tall
at all.
One day he is going to take a fall
in the hall
while wearing a shawl
that he got from John Paul
as he cuddled a doll
named Saul
that he got at the mall
last fall.
He has a lot of gall
and he is going to call
out
"I've fallen and I can't get up,
ya'll."

Raven has a cravin'
She wants an omelet real bad.
I can't remember what Malia got,
But it came with toast.
Malia didn't want the toast,
So she gave it to Lori.
Lori didn't order nothing.
Nothing at all,
just coffee.
Oh wait, didn't she order yogurt?
Yeah, I think she did.

But I don't think she ate it
She just ate the toast Malia gave her
And drank her coffee.
Why would you order yogurt
but not eat it?
Who does that? That's seriously fucked up.
Hey Lori, stay out of the Honky Tonks.
We don't serve your precious yogurt here.

Raven has a cravin'
She wants an omelet real bad.
The name of the restaurant we went to
Was Pancho and Lefty's
which is the name of a Willie Nelson song
that goes on really long.
If he ever sang it for Chuck Barris
He would probably get the gong
And then go smoke a bong
with Tommy Chong
and Shelly Long
from Cheers.

Raven has a cravin'
She wants an omelet real bad.
A waffle is what I had.
It was good.

Jim Larsen

Jenny's Placenta Tree

Jenny's placenta
Is magenta.
It's buried in the earth,
Planted there with glee
Planted there with mirth,
A byproduct of giving birth.

Jenny's placenta
in the earth.

Jenny's placenta is in the ground
She dug a hole there on the mound,
And placed it there without a sound.
Jenny's placenta on the mound.

Placenta
Placenta
Jenny's placenta

From it, a tree will grow.
What kind of tree?
Oh, I don't know.

A mango tree
Or a papaya tree,
Any kind of tree
that you can see.

Something with fruit to share.
A placenta tree
Oh so rare.

Placenta tree
Placenta tree,
Eat the fruit of the placenta tree
And you'll grow strong
Just like me.

Placenta tree
Oh, placenta tree
From you
We can even make some tea.

Placenta tea
Placenta tea

If you make tea
From the placenta tree
Please, please, please
Share with me.

No matter what the cost,
I'll pay the fee.
I sure love placenta tea.

Placenta trees
Placenta trees,
The whole world needs
Placenta trees.

If more women
Would bury their placenta after birth,
Then placenta trees would cover the earth.

Cover the earth,
Cover the earth,
One day placenta trees
Will rule the earth.

Jim Larsen

Bacon in the Pig Slop 2.0

Where did all the bacon go?
You guys used to love us so,
You put bacon in the pig slop
Two, three times a week.
Now our spirits have grown so weak.
No longer do we dance with glee,
Because there's no more bacon.

No more bacon.
No more bacon.
No more bacon in the pig slop.
Why'd you stop?

There's still Gorilla Munch
To give it crunch
But no more honey to make it sweet.
If I were the president, I'd send an angry tweet.
Because there's no more bacon.
No more bacon.
No more bacon in the Pig Slop.
Why'd you stop?

Did you see we liked it so?
And so you said, "Oh, no, no, no.
No happy pigs,
Not around here.
We've had enough of you
For this year.

So no more bacon.
No more bacon.
No more bacon in the pig slop.
We had to stop.

You pigs were too happy.
You were over the top.

Fat Naked Poetry

We need to keep you in your place.
Don't want to see no smiles on your face.
So now breakfast is lentils, chards, beans and rice.
Don't complain.
Hey, ain't that nice?

A boiled egg, or maybe two,
More than that's not good for you.

But no more bacon.
No more bacon.
No more bacon in the pig slop.
We had to stop."

Walking

Walking down the road
wishing I could fly.
I want to go home
but I'm too afraid to die.

So I'm walking.
That's right I'm just walking.
Just walking down this road.

Walking down the road
wishing I could fly.
I want to go home
but it ain't my turn to die.

So I'm walking.
Just walking.
Walking down this road.

You're only going to live
live until you die.
I had to clip your wings
so now you can't fly.

Now you gotta keep on walking.
Keep on walking down this road.
You want to go home
but you're too afraid to die.

I had to clip your wings
so now you can't fly.
You want to get to Heaven
but you're too afraid to die.

Keep on walking.
Walking down this road.

The Apocalypse is Now

Don't eat the skin the lizard shed,
 it does no good it's already dead.
 If you want to stay alive, you need flesh that's still alive.
The apocalypse is now.

As you cravings start to change,
the feelings you feel will seem strange.
Don't judge yourself for wanting brains.
It's what you are now.
You've eaten your last cow.

Your kind is spreading
this is where the world is heading.
You really should be fretting.
Soon you are all the same,
but where oh where is the blame?

Started with one and then became two
before you knew it, it spread to you.
Each and every all the same
but I ask again, who's to blame?

Don't eat the skin the lizard shed.
It's still no good, it's already dead.
Watch the others what they do
and then you can do it too.
We have become each all the same.
Perhaps the media is to blame.
The apocalypse is now.

Judgment

Sometimes I remind myself that I shouldn't judge other people, but then I think, if I don't judge other people, then how do I know who I am better than?

Forbidden Black Rick

I'm not the doctor,
And I'm not the nurse.
I'm just the guy who drives the hearse.
But when the doctor fails,
And the nurse does too,
Then they'll call me to come get you.

My name is Rick.
Forbidden Black Rick.

Nobody likes it when I come to town.
They all get nervous when I'm around.
Who am I here for?
They all want to know.
Is it their dad?
Their mom?
Their cousin Joe?

I carry their dead.
I get them and go
To the graveyard.
It's not that hard to do.
It wasn't for them,
It won't be for you.

My name is Rick.
They call me
Forbidden Black Rick.

Nobody likes to see my face.
It's not about creed
It's not about race.
They see me and they all want to hide.
Because I don't come around
Unless somebody's died.

Jim Larsen

I drive a big car
It's shiny and black
With plenty of room
For you in the back.

They see me
And they all get a chill
As I inch my way
Up Cemetery Hill.

I'm not the doctor,
And I'm not the nurse.
I'm just the guy who drives the hearse.

I'm just me
Here doing my job.
I've come to fetch your Uncle Bob.

Your Uncle Bob lived a really nice life.
He didn't cause sadness
He didn't cause strife
He always brought gladness
He never brought hurt.
But now that I have him,
Let's cover him with dirt.

I'm not the doctor,
And I'm not the nurse.
I'm just the guy who drives the hearse.

My name is Rick.
You may call me
Forbidden Black Rick.

Lament for a Sad Egg

I'm just an egg.
A sad and simple egg.
An egg who is all alone.
But I want people to like me.
I want you to like me
Or else I died in vain.
Please cook me in a fancy way
Not something simple and plain.

I want to make people happy.
I need to make people happy!
So please give me half a chance
To make people love me
And want to get up and dance.

I'm just an egg.
A sad and lonely egg
But filled with potential and style.
But nobody loves a boiled egg
So please don't make me a boiled egg
If you boil me, I'll break your leg.

There's no love in a boiled egg.
It takes no talent to make a boiled egg
Please, please, please don't make me beg.
I don't want to be a boiled egg.
I don't want to be boiled egg.
So find a fun recipe for me in your file.

Let me be a tasty egg
Everybody loves a tasty egg
Scramble me with cheese
Or make me fried egg
Please, please, please don't make me beg.
Put me in an omelet
As a happy egg.
Everybody loves a frittata egg

Jim Larsen

And I'm an egg who needs some love.
And nobody loves a boiled egg.
Boiled eggs are hard to peel.
People would rather eat a rat lung
or an eel.

Nobody loves a boiled egg.
Nobody loves a boiled egg.
Please, please don't make me beg.
I don't want to be a boiled egg.
I don't want to be a boiled egg.
I'm just an egg.

A sad and simple egg.
An egg who is all alone.
An egg who is so alone.

Hippy Sweat on the Dance Floor

T'was Sunday Morning in Puna
and a goodly crowd was there
that well nigh filled the Emax Center
with plenty of hippies to spare.

They gathered there, as they every weekend do
for a church service that may seem strange
unless you do it too.
"Ecstatic Dance" is the name somebody gave it.

The dance was the dance that was the dance
and the dancers danced with glee.

Then it was time for the invocation and everybody sat down. Well, I shouldn't say everybody sat down, because not everybody did sit down, some people laid down. That's right, laid down- stretched out on the Ecstatic Dance room floor.

The invocation invocated, it was time to dance again.
The music played and bodies swayed, and the dancers got to their feet.

They leapt and jumped and yelled, all to the bumping beat
in worship to their gods on high
when what did I spy with my little eye,
but a mess that somebody made!

Hippy sweat on the dance floor
somebody should mop that up.
A brilliant sight in the morning light,
a gleam, a shimmer, a puddle, a smear.
Hippy sweat on the dance floor!
And there are children present here!

Children are those with impressionable minds
they don't know proper from bad.
They see a puddle on the floor
they think, "Wow! There is some fun to be had!"

Jim Larsen

A running start, running start
A Hawaiian slip and slide!

Hippy sweat on the dance floor.
Please, somebody mop that up.

The two go together,
this I know-
Sweat and the dance.
But glimmering there
in the ecstatic air
that's too much of a chance.
You could slip on it and bust your head open.

Hippy sweat on the dance floor-
am I the only one concerned?
Seriously, friends
let's not pretend
that you don't see it too.

An oil slick of the hippy kind
just waiting for you to slip.
Just waiting for you to slip.

Hippy sweat on the dance floor.
My sweat is on there too.

Forgiveness

I don't think it's a good idea to pray for forgiveness because what if God wasn't paying attention when you did whatever it is you did? Then all you're doing is telling on yourself.

Jim Larsen

I Don't Mind

I don't mind getting herpes
if I get them form you.
I don't mind gonorrhea
the itching burning goo.
I don't mind getting crabs
they can crawl on me like ants,
if that's what it takes to get into your pants.

I don't mind.
No, I don't mind.
You're such a sexy lady
I don't mind.

If you got a case of the syphilis,
I really don't care.
If you got genital warts
I promise not to stare.
If you have inflammation
on your private parts down there
I won't let it bother me
because that would not be fair.

I don't mind,
no I don't mind.
Whatever you got,
baby I'll get it too
if that's what it takes
to spend the night with you.

The Easter Bunny

Here comes Peter Cotton Tail Fleeing down the Bunny Trail.
Hibbidy-Hobbidy the Wolf is after you.
Think of all the girls and boys
who will be so annoyed
If they don't have chocolate Easter Morning.

Run Run Peter Cotton Tail
Faster down the Bunny trail
The wolf is hungry
he hasn't eaten in a while.
If he's able to catch you
you know just what he'll do
he'll eat you whole and leave your guts there in a pile.

There comes a time in every man's life when he must reflect and examine the life he has lived, finding answers to the questions that race through his mind. "Have I lived a life that is noble and good? Have the decisions I made supported my own best good and the highest good of others? What should I have done differently? What did I do right?

With the hot breath of the wolf bearing down on him, the Easter Bunny, delirious with his own inner turmoil, saw a million questions flash. So many questions, so heavy with doubt, plaguing his very soul. Do children really need sugar-loaded jelly beans? Don't colored Easter eggs just create a false reality for impressionable young minds? Is it the right thing to steal the glory of Easter from Jesus?

You see, there comes a time in every man's life when he has no choice but to stand and face his demons. You can't outrun them, and you can't hide from them either. Oh, you can try to hide, but they know where you're at. And run? Ha! However fast you think you are, the Devil's a whole lot faster. You know that, right? Right?

Right now we see the Easter Bunny. He's running as fast as his four little lucky rabbits feet will take him. Let's hope they're as lucky as they're fabled to be.

Jim Larsen

Easter Bunny you better run to save your life
Hell's broke loose on the bunny trail
and the wolf's teeth are sharper than a knife
If you run fast enough you get to live another day
But if you slow down the wolf will have his way.

There goes Peter Cotton Tail
eaten on the bunny trail
Hibbidy-Hobbidy the Wolf caught up to you.
I guess you ran just too slow
was it meant to be?
I don't know
But now who will bring the chocolate Easter Morning?
Who will bring the chocolate Easter morning?

Bovine Teet Excretion

Shakespeare said, "A rose by any other name is still a rose." The same can be said of milk. Milk is just as milky whether you call it "Milk" or if you call it "Bovine Teet Excretion."

"Hey Jim, how do you like to eat an Oreo Cookie?"
"I like to dunk my Oreo Cookie in a nice cold glass of Bovine Teet Excretion."

Another good word for butter is "Chunky Bovine Teet Excretion." If that ever caught on though, you know there would be an imitation product called "I Can't Believe it's not Chunky Bovine Teet Excretion."

I like to eat my popcorn with nice hot Chunky Bovine Teet Excretion melted over it.

What do Tibetans love to drink? Why, Chunky Bovine Teet Excretion Tea, of course.

Death Song

Woke up in the morning
expecting a good day.
But what can I say?
It didn't go that way.
I have tickets to a play.
I should have just given them away
because I won't make it now.
How can I make it now?
I won't live another minute.
No, not another minute
with this girl killing me.
Oh, why is she killing me?
I don't even know her name,
but she hates me all the same.
I don't deserve to die.
Woke up in the morning
expecting a good day.
I should have just gone back to bed,
because now I'm...

Dead.

Moon Over Sara 2: Menopause

Hide Hide Hide
Sara no longer hides.
Sara no longer hides from the moon.
Her ovaries, they had a good run.
She has a daughter and a son
But now her birthing days are done.
But that's okay.
She can still have her fun.
She's hit menopause.

Hide Hide Hide
Sara no longer hides.
Sara no longer hides from the moon.
Moon cycles
Sara's cycles.
Sara no longer cycles with the moon.

Her final cycle was last June.
She will discover that real soon
That she no longer cycles with the moon.
Sara's going through "The change."
Which is why she's acting so awfully strange.
Her emotions certainly do run the range
From irrational to completely insane.

Because like a flash
Forward dash
She had
What we call
A hot flash.
And no longer cycles with the moon.

Moon Moon Moon
Now she cycles with a different moon.
Now she sings a different tune.
Moon Moon Moon
Sara no longer feels the moon.

Jim Larsen

Hey diddle diddle
The cat and the fiddle
Can you solve the riddle
The riddle of Sara's womb?

Sara's womb
Is now a tomb
A tomb for the moon
The moon of Sarah's cycle.

Cycle Cycle Cycle
Sara no longer cycles.
Sara no longer cycles with the moon.

Old Sweaty C

Everybody sweats
this much is true.
But I know somebody who sweats more than me
sweats more than you.
He's a friend of mine
from far across the sea.
He goes by the name "Old Sweaty C."

He's a landscaper by trade
and he likes to pull weeds.
He'll weed in the garden
he'll weed under trees.
He'll weed all day under the hot summer sun.
When there's no more weeds
his work will be done.

He's got dirt on his shirt
And dirt in his eye.
He's got dirt on his underwear
because he unzipped his fly.
That's how he rolls.
You never question the methods
of Old Sweaty C.

Old Sweaty C
Beautifying the aina for you and me.
Wipe the sweat from your eye
So you can see.
There's more weeds to pull
Old Sweaty C.

From Mauka to Makai
From mountain to sea,
make sure you get them all
Old Sweaty C.

Your shirt is drenched
and so is your hat.

Jim Larsen

There's a puddle of sweat
where you just sat.
You better replenish
your electrolytes
Old Sweaty C.

All this sweat
is starting to worry me.
Why do you sweat so much
Old Sweaty C?
It's not natural for a man to
Sweat like you do.

But that's how you are
what God intended for you.
He made some of us handsome
he made some of us fat.
He made you all sweaty
and that is just that.

Keep doing what you do
Old Sweaty C.

The One I Need

I got one in my bed,
and one on my mind.
I got two more, they're knocking at my door
Uh-Huh, oh yeah, that's right.

Now Jenny June, she's a mighty fine gal
I like her a lot, she is my pal.
She cooks and she cleans and she vacuums too,
but no big deal because so does Sue.
Uh-huh, oh yeah, that's right.

I got one in my bed,
and one on my mind.
I got two more, they're knocking at my door.
I got women, so many women,
everyone but the one I need.

Now Suzie Marie
needs to go so I can be free.
She's sweet and she's cute
but she talks too much,
so she gets the boot.
Uh-huh, oh yeah, that's right.

Now Linda May, she is okay.
I met her just the other day.
She's really smart
and she's really neat.
She almost swept me off my feet.
Uh-huh, oh yeah, that's right.

Well, the one on my mind is the one I need,
but she's gone gone gone.
The one on mind is the one I need,
but she's gone gone gone.
The one on my mind is the one I need.
She's really great,
she is indeed,

Jim Larsen

but she's gone gone gone.
Uh-huh, oh yeah, that's right.

Blind Lady on the Metro

One time I was on the Washington DC metro, an old blind woman sat in the seat next to me. I didn't particularly want an old blind woman sitting next to me that day, so I flipped her off. In time, the futility of flipping a person off who could not see that they were being flipped off occurred to me, so I took her hand and placed it on my hand so that she could use the sense of touch to take in the fact that she was being flipped off. It seemed to bother her a great deal, but I didn't have time to fight with her because the metro got to my stop and I had to go.

Fleeting

Fleeting.
through the forest
in the mist
down the road.
Fleeting.

The first raindrop lights atop my head
deteriorating my senses
leaving me achingly dull.
The gravel is bigger in this part of town.
You know what I mean.

This world of sunbaked clams,
the surface is foul.
I will not raise my children here.
Mary Tyler Moore would though,
all of them.

Searching for Plato's perfect waffle,
it seems that the highway should end soon
before the illumination becomes absurd,
like a tree with too many corn stalks growing in its trunk.
Yes.

Paper was thinner when I was your age,
and "brother" meant the other male offspring of your parents.
I have a question
that only you can answer.
Whatever.

We should see light soon
this plane can't fly forever
with so many bounced checks
occupying its seats.
Forever.

When it is all over

and I am no more,
let them say this of me:
may he rest in this,
God's wonderful earth
for good this time.

Jim Larsen

Waiting for Toast

She waits for her toast.
Is the toaster plugged in?
Oh wait, it is not.

Old Man Waiting for a Bus

Beard of white
a man well dressed
his eyes kind gentle and wise.
The turban on his head
reflects is truth
it's not a costume or disguise.

It's you I see as we drive by you wait there for your bus. An unintended glance reveals the truth
you're just like the rest of us.

Old man waiting for the bus I see you scratching your balls.
Old man waiting for the bus
It's something we all do.
When I have an itch you know I scratch it too.

It's my first trip to India My first time in New Delhi. A stranger in this land.

Old man you remind me of my
own truth the human race is one great band.

Old man when you're scratching your balls
you know you're scratching
mine too.
You know you're scratching
mine too.

We're all just one. We're all the same. If you know that,
you've won the game.

Old man scratching his balls on the street
thank you for being you. Old man scratching his balls on the street
thank you for being true.

Namaste.

Jim Larsen

Flo's Fever Down There

Do you know Flo
the way I know Flo?
If you know Flo
the way I know Flo
then you know
that Flo
has a fever down there.

A fever down where?
A fever down there.
In her underwear.

Flow has a fever
that burns in her beaver-
a euphemistic word for vagina.

Her doctors swear it's angina
that she picked up in China.
But I say no!
They don't know Flo
the way I know Flo.

For if they knew Flo
the way I know Flo
Then they would know
her fever is a desire-
a desire to sire
an entire
family of Appalachian Hill-Folke.

Flo is a little strange that way.
Strange what way?
Strange like she's gay?
No, I didn't say
she was gay.
I know that Flo does not sway that way.

All I said was that she is peculiar.
Flo has a fever.
It burns in her beaver-
a euphemistic word for vagina.
A euphemistic word for vagina.
Join me in some talk story-
talk story about Flo's fever down there.

Jim Larsen

Coconut Head

Coconut Head
Coconut Head
Just be thankful you're not dead
There are a lot worse things than going through life with a coconut for your head
Coconut Head.

An accident with a great big knife
you lost your head
but I saved your life
Coconut Head.

Stuffed your brain in a coconut shell
just to keep you safe from Hell.
Cost less than a bushel
less than a peck
to put that coconut back on your neck
Coconut Head.

You're not the man you used to be
that is very plain to see.
I drew your eyes with a Sharpee pen
Just so you could see again
Coconut Head.

Look in the mirror
and what do you see?
A freakish thing from a coconut tree?
Does this make you feel angry?
What would you have done if you were me?
Just left you to die, set your spirit free
Coconut Head?

Coconut Head
Coconut Head
I'm sorry you start each day with dread.
Could it be you'd be happier dead
than facing the world with a coconut for your head?

Coconut Head.

I understand you want a wife
but Coconut Head
put down that knife.
You can't have her just like you
that ain't the right thing to do
Coconut Head.

Coconut Head
Coconut Head
Now are you all stained and red.
Who's that woman in your bed?
Didn't you hear what I said?
The world doesn't need a lady
Coconut Head.

Promise me if you have a daughter
or if you have a son
you'll let them be
to have their fun.
You won't be a family on the run
hiding from the world
with coconuts for your heads
Coconut Head.

Jim Larsen

Nicky the Slut

Once I was a slut Just a poor and lonely slut. I would sleep with any guy.
Any fat and slavish guy.
Oh me oh me oh my.

As long as he paid me money. It didn't have to be much money.
As long as he had some money.
A quarter or a nickel would do.
That's what I used to do.

But now I've changed And now I'm different.
I don't roll that way no more.
Don't you dare call me a whore
Because I'm not a whore
Not any more.

Now I am a killer- A viscous evil killer.
Oh why am I a killer?

How did I become a killer? Something evil's inside of me.
Oh golly gee.

I just want them to die.
I can't say why.

I want this evil gone from me!

Once I was a slut Just a poor and lonely slut.
It wasn't a good life
But it was a life I understood.

It was a life I understood.
Who am I know?

Ode to Gluten

Gluten, Gluten
Oh how I love gluten.
I love it in my pie
I love it in my cake
I love to have gluten
in everything I bake.
Gluten is good!
Gluten is good!
So grab a spoon and have some flour with me.

Gluten, Gluten
Let's all eat gluten.
No gluten allergy
can ever bother me
and it cannot bother you
unless you want it to
because there's no such thing.
It's all in your head.

Gluten, Gluten
the whole world loves gluten.
Only an absolute sissy
would ask for gluten free
so grow a pair and have some bread with me.

Gluten, Gluten
The universe loves gluten.
Gluten is great!
Gluten is great!
It is a gift from God.

Jim Larsen

Bubble Bath

I like my bubble bath
All those bubbles make me laugh.
Ha ha ha. Hee hee ho.
Fill up my tub and away I go.

Be careful that it's not
way too cold
or much too hot
that's a lesson I've been taught
soaking in my bubble bath.
You can put that on my epitaph.

A bubble hat
and a bubble beard
You just might think I'm weird.
But that's okay, I don't mind
A better time you'll never find.
I am so filled with glee
when bubbles are all I see.
Rubber Ducky floating by
just dropped in, to say hi.

"Hi Jim! How's it going?"
"It's going great, Rubber Ducky!"
"Glad to hear it, Jim!"
"Rubber Ducky, you're my friend. I love you."
"Aw Jim, I love you too."
I love my bubble bath.
All those bubbles make me laugh.
Time to get out now
I should go.
I'm starting to get a wrinkled toe.
"Goodbye Rubber Ducky!"
"Goodbye Jim! See you next time!"

Bubble bath, bubble bath. Bubble bubble bubble bath.
Bubble bath, bubble bath. I love you because you make me laugh.

Food Nerd

I am a big sissy
who only eats gluten free.
I am a great big dork
who will not eat pork.
I say no to beef
it gets stuck in my teeth.

I don't know if you've heard
I'm nothing but a big food nerd.

Food nerd
food nerd
food nerd.
I'm picky about what I eat.
Food nerd
food nerd
food nerd
I'm totally afraid of meat.

I won't touch no scrambled eggs
they will lead to gouty legs.
I'll take one if it's boiled though.
What's the difference?
I don't know.

Eat a chicken
and you'll burn in Hell.
How about tofu?
Oh, that stuff's swell.

If it's not peanut free
don't you dare feed it to me.
If it has sugar in it
I'll sit right here and throw a fit
.
That's just how I am.
My allergies are not a scam.

Jim Larsen

I think by now you may have heard
I'm nothing but a big food nerd.

Food nerd
food nerd
food nerd.
Dairy products make me shudder.
Food nerd
food nerd
food nerd.
I cant's eat anything from an udder.

Food nerd
food nerd
food nerd
I won't eat anything cooked in lard.
Food nerd
food nerd
food nerd
But man oh man I love that chard.

Food nerd
food nerd
food nerd

I don't know if you've heard
I'm sure by now you've probably heard
Don't you think it's so absurd
I'm nothing but a big food nerd.

A Good Charlie Brown Special Idea

A good Charlie brown Special would be one where Charlie Brown and the whole Peanuts gang are crossing a treacherous mountain pass and the blizzard of the century kicks up leaving them stranded with precious little supplies and absolutely no food. Somehow, some way Charlie Brown becomes the unofficial leader of the group and he is forced to make the difficult decision that in order to stay alive, they must sacrifice Linus to have food to sustain them until the thaw comes and they could get off that God-forsaken mountain.

So that's what they do, they butcher Linus, manage to make a fire, cook him, and consume his flesh to keep themselves alive. Then the snow melts a few days later and they get to where they were going. Then, the special is really about Charlie Brown coping with the trauma of having cannibalized his best, and some would argue, only friend. Sure, Linus would call Charlie Brown a "Block Head" but he called him that with an irony that can only be appreciated by true, life-long friends.

Charlie Brown is never the same after the mountain experience. Not even frequent visits to Lucy's psychiatric booth could help him find the inner peace he lost in that blizzard snow and hell. So, finally, on Halloween night, out in the Pumpkin Patch where he laughed so many times at Linus for waiting for The great Pumpkin to appear and declare his patch the most sincere, drunk and hopped up on crystal meth, Charlie Brown, with a Smith and Wesson taken from Schroeder's dad's gun cabinet, blows his own brains out.

The name of that Charlie Brown Special could be, "You'd Still be Alive Today if Schroeder's Dad had Locked the Gun Cabinet, Charlie Brown."

Jim Larsen

A Poem about Ultraman

Ultraman, Ultraman
Thinks he's better than the average man.
Can he swing
from a thread?
If he tried,
We'd all be dead.
He's too big for that, he's like 90 feet tall,
He's Ultraman.

Ultraman, Ultraman,
he was born in Japan
Did you know his real name is Dan?
But only his close friends call him that. Unless he tells you otherwise, you better just call him Ultraman.

Ultraman Ultraman
He's a John Bon Jovie fan.
His favorite song is Shot through the heart and your to blame
but to me his songs all sound the same
but that's just me, I'm not Ultraman.

Ultraman Ultraman
He's a member of the Ku Klux Klan.
He won't like you
if your skin is black
but if you're white, he's got your back.
He's very racist and that's not cool,
he's Ultraman.

Do you know? Do you know?
Who killed all of the buffalo?
The used to roam on the plain
but now it seems they've all been slain
It wasn't me,
it was Ultraman.

Hey hey hey,

hey hey hey.
Don't get hit by his Spacium Ray.
Nebula M78 is home
Nebula M78 is home to Ultraman.

Ultraman Ultraman
likes the beach,
so he's always tan.
He can swim
really fast
even with his leg
in a cast.
Is that a whale coming at us?
No, it's Ultraman.

Ultraman Ultraman
likes to fry things in a pan.
Fried chicken
French Fries
Onion Rings
I tell no lies-
No lies!
About Ultraman.

Now you know
Now you know
Everything there is to know.
Everything there is to know-
about Ultraman.

Jim Larsen

Jesus Saves. So does David Hasselhoff.

I saw a bumper sticker that said "Jesus Saves." You know who else saves? David Hasselhoff. He was a lifeguard on Baywatch. If you are drowning out in the ocean, David Hasselhoff will save you. If you are drowning in sin, Jesus will save you. But what if you are sinning out in the ocean? Then, the race is on. Who is going to get to you first? My money would be on Jesus, because he can run across the water, but I don't know. David Hasselhoff is a strong swimmer. Whatever the results are though, I know the fans will get their money's worth.

Dating Advice

There is one thing that I get asked a lot, and that is, "Jim, can you please give us some dating advice so we can be popular with the ladies, just like you are?" My answer is, "Yes I can."

Here it is- My step by step guide to being popular with the ladies.

1. Starting Conversations.

First of all, and this is probably the most important to keep in mind, it is NOT up to you to start a conversation. It's up to her, and if she fails to say anything interesting in the first twenty minutes of the date, then it's okay for you to get up and leave. Life is short. Remember that. You don't want to waste one precious minute sitting around with a girl who isn't going to say anything good. You don't have to explain yourself and you don't even have to say goodbye. Just get up and go.

2. Find out her Zodiac Sign

Find out as soon as possible what her zodiac sign is. As clichéd and corny as this may sound, it serves an important purpose. If she says that she is a Capricorn, end it with her right then and there. Just walk away and don't look back. Capricorns, ALL Capricorns were conceived in a lake of fire with the single goal of dragging you back to Hell with them. Do you need that?

3. Compliment Her

For some reason, girls like to be complimented. There is something about external validation that sparks within them a heightened state of arousal. If there is nothing obvious about them to say anything good about, compliment them on their feet. For example, you could say, "You got nice feet. It's cool how symmetrically proportionate they are to each other." Another area to target is the face. You might want to say, "I like how symmetrical your eyes are to each other." Or, "You sure got a purdy mouth."

4. Give her Chocolate

It's important to keep in mind that all girls everywhere like chocolate. Therefore, it is to your ultimate benefit to carry a bag of Hershey's Kisses with you. Be careful though that your date does not eat more than two or she will get fat, and that will make it that much harder to find something to compliment her on.

5. Make Eye Contact

Girls feel comforted and safe with you as long as you maintain eye contact with them. I suggest while you're waiting for them to start a conversation, you look in them in the eyes and hold their gaze as long as you can without blinking.

6. Ask her Name

Sometimes the date might be going fine, but you find you simply can't remember her name, which is to be expected because there is something like four billion names that it might be, so how are you supposed to remember the one that it is? In this case, just ask her. Say, "What did you say your name was again?" Ask her this as many times as it takes for you to remember. "What did you say your name was again?" The girl will appreciate the effort and it will show that you really care.

7. Take an Interest in her Family

Finally, girls dig it when you take an interest in their family. One way to do this is to make inquiries about her father. Ask her, "Who's your daddy? Who's your daddy? Who's your daddy?"

And that's all you really need to know. Master these things and you too shall be popular with the ladies, just like I am.

Cautionary Tale

Mothers please listen to me
about where to breastfeed your baby.
There's a time and a place
but if you want to stay safe
stay away from the coconut tree.

The story I tell now is true.
Don't let it happen to you.
It happened to Mary
and her baby, Little Larry
but prevention's so easy to do.

T'was a calm happy day near here
as Mary walked home with good cheer.
Her baby in her arm
she intended no harm
wanting to get home to have a cold beer.

The baby, it started to cry
and Mary knew exactly just why.
His face turning red
he wanted to be fed
so Mary sat down with a huge sigh.

She should have been more careful where she sat
but her bosom was becoming quite fat
as it filled up with milk
against her blouse made of silk
she sat down beneath a coconut tree.

Take caution near coconut trees.
Coconuts are heavy and prone to gravity.
If one falls on your head
you'll end up quite dead
just like this Mother Mary.

When it happened, it happened quite quick.

Jim Larsen

The sight of it would make you real sick.
A coconut fell
sent Mary to Hell
but Baby Larry didn't suffer one lick.

That's why the baby still fed.
He didn't know that his mother was dead.
He sucked on her tit
still getting milk out of it
to a false sense of security is where he was led.

But soon the flow of milk did stop.
No more would the mammary produce.
He sucked and he sucked
feeling quite stuck
as his mother's flesh turned as cold as a goose.

Hunger soon gripped the poor child
not created to feed in the wild.
The lack of lactation
gave him a heart palpitation
ending a life so sweet and so mild.

The locals still point out the tree
where they say they still see Mother Mary
a ghostly apparition
still providing nutrition
from her breast to her baby Larry.

Mothers, I hope you heard well.
When you feel your breast start to swell.
You can breastfeed anywhere
but please do take care not to do it beneath a coconut tree.

Pretty Girls on the Metro

Sometimes when I ride the metro, there's nothing better to do than to stare at the back of the head of the person in the seat in front of me. So if I'm lucky, it will be a really pretty girl with really clean hair, shiny hair that doesn't have any lint stuck in it or anything like that. And maybe if I'm really lucky, she will turn her head just enough for me to get a good look at her reflection in the window. And if I'm really really lucky, she'll be really pretty. That way,

I can....

 fantasize...

...about what it would be like if she married my dad and become my new mom. Then maybe she'd take me shopping and buy me new shoes and stuff and maybe she has a great recipe for lasagna that she will cook for me on my birthday. I've seen a lot of pretty girls that my dad should get married to. He's been lonely since mom went to work in the liquor store.

Jim Larsen

What Makes You Stronger

They say, "What doesn't kill you only makes you stronger." Yeah, but what if you could bench press four hundred pounds, but then you lose both your arms in a chainsaw accident. That's not going to make you stronger. That's just going to make you sad.

Throwing Fish at Tammy

I'm throwing fish at Tammy
While hiding in a tree.
This fish is charred
it's way to hard
that can't be good for me.
So I'm throwing fish at Tammy
while hiding in a tree.

Tammy cooks our meals for us
she cooks them every day.
99 out of 100 taste real good
but number 100, what can I say?
She needs to know
so up a tree I go
to send her my critique
this is my mystique.
That it's me, she'll never know.

I'm throwing scrambled eggs at Tammy
while hiding in a tree.
These eggs are runny
and that's not funny
they just seem gross to me.
So I'm throwing eggs at Tammy
while hiding in a tree.

Tammy is a real great girl
who loves to do her part.
She cooks, she bakes, she makes great cakes
she has an amazing heart.
But perfection is hard to achieve
which I know is hard to believe
so I have a trick up my sleeve
about where I can go to heave
the pies that taste too tart.

I'm throwing pie at Tammy
while hiding in a tree.

Jim Larsen

It's an apple pie
and that is why
because I prefer cherry.
So I'm throwing pie at Tammy
while hiding in a tree.

I'm pouring soup on Tammy
while hiding in a tree.
This soup's too hot
and that is not
how I like it to be.
So I'm pouring soup on Tammy
while hiding in a tree.

I'm flinging oatmeal at Tammy
while hiding in a tree.
This oatmeal is soupy
which drives me loopy
and it ruins all my glee.
So I'm flinging oatmeal at Tammy
while hiding in a tree.

I'm throwing food at Tammy
while hiding in a tree.

Rome

They say Rome wasn't built in a day, but parts of it had to have been.

Sarcasm

Sometimes I think that maybe sarcasm is wasted on stupid people because stupid people are too dumb to realize they are being sarcasmed against. So if I am never sarcastic with you, it just means I don't think much of you.

Better Butter

You need better butter
for better batter
But not too much
or you'll get fatter.

Butter?
Butter.
Bitty bits of bitter butter
squeezed straight out of that cow's udder.

You heard me
Did I Stutter? Bitty bits of butter.
Who's butter?
What butter? Her butter?
Not her butter, but her butter
Butter butter, is it so?
Why ask me, I don't know.

Whatever happened to Larry Mondello?
He was Beaver's friend.
It was supposed to be till the end.
But then he disappeared
and Whitey joined the show.
And I don't know,
it just wasn't the same.
Why did you go,
Larry Mondello?

You need better butter
for better batter
but not too much
or you'll get fatter.
But not too much
or we'll all get fatter.

Jim Larsen

Yoga Poser

You bend down and touch your toes
but I wouldn't call that a yoga pose.
You think your yoga's really hot
I hate to tell you this-
it's not.

You don't know yoga
and yoga don't know you.
Is that a head stand you're trying to do?
Shit, man. Why don't you just sit your ass down.
You call yourself a yogi
but you look more like a clown.

You're worse than a Canadian hoser.
You're a yoga poser.

Your downward dog looks like a bitch
who taught you that Eagle Pose?
Lilo and Stich?

You can't even take a deep breath and then say "Om."
I see a light on
but there ain't nobody home.

Your warrior pose just lost the fight
Can you even do a hip opener
without getting uptight?
Your dolphin pose is the chicken of the sea
and what is that pose supposed to be?

You forward lunge just like a bulldozer
You're a yoga poser.

You lie down in corpse pose
and Riga mortise sets in
do you always twitch like that?
Or should I call your next of kin?

You go into child's pose all gloomy and glum
like a three year old
having some big tantrum.

Your rabbit pose should just hop out of town.
And that tree pose of yours?
Dude, just chop it down.

So go ahead then
touch your toes.
You can call that a yoga pose
if that's really the best you can do
but you know what?
I kind of feel sorry for you.

Because you're worse than a tone deaf composer.
You're a yoga poser.

Oreos

Bread is used to symbolize the flesh of Christ, but maybe it is time to update that idea for the 21st century and use Oreo Cookies to represent the flesh of Christ instead. That would be cool. If we did that, and I was one of Jesus' apostles, I would turn to one of the other apostles and say, "Hey man, how do you eat the flesh of Christ?" And he'd say, "I always eat the creamy center of Christ first." And I'd say, "I like to dip my Christ in milk." And then he'd ask what's in Mud Pie ice cream, and I would tell him it has coffee flavored ice cream with big chunks of Jesus in it.

Chainsaw Boy

Chainsaw Boy
Chainsaw Boy
Is that saw your favorite toy?
Why does it bring you so much joy?
Help us understand you,
Chainsaw Boy.

Chainsaw Boy thinks he's a man
clearing trees on our land.
Thanks for giving us a hand
but your work's all done now, Chainsaw Boy.
Time to go home now, Chainsaw Boy.
Why are you still here, Chainsaw Boy?
Please just go, Chainsaw Boy.

Chainsaw Boy knows his trees.
He can tell you about everyone he sees.
He seperates the good ones from the weeds
but can you take a hint from that, Chainsaw Boy?
Do you really belong here, Chainsaw Boy?
What do you want from us, Chainsaw Boy?
Are you ever going to go, Chainsaw Boy?

Chainsaw Boy works day and night.
His hero complex
is our plight.
Here you are
and there you go,
just how big is your ego?

Do you think that we are impressed
that you plan to be undressed?
naked at the pool, Chainsaw Boy?
Just keep your mouth shut, Chainsaw Boy.
Keep it in your pants, Chainsaw Boy.
Nobody cares, Chainsaw Boy.

Jim Larsen

Chainsaw Boy likes to play
but are you straight
or are you gay?
Or is it that you sway either way?
We have to ask
because it's hard to say.
What is your story, Chainsaw Boy?
We're trying to understand you, Chainsaw Boy.
Meet us half way here, Chainsaw Boy.

Chainsaw Boy, it's time to go.
We appreciate your work,
don't you know.
But enough is enough
and that is that.
See you next time,
Chainsaw Boy.

The Truth About Santa

You better watch out
You better watch out
You better watch out
You better watch out
You better watch out
Santa Claus is coming to your house.

He knows where your home is.
He knows which house is yours.
Locking the door won't help because he can evade every security system known to man.
Fa-la-la-la-la-la

You better not pout
You better not pout
You better not pout
You better not pout
Santa Claus is waiting for you right now.

He'll bring you lots of presents,
but nothing that you want.
He forgot what you asked for
but never really cared anyway.

You better be good
You better be good

He sees you when you're sleeping.
He knows when you're asleep.
He enjoys seeing the steady, rhythmic rising and falling of your chest as you breath in and out in your peaceful slumber time.

You might wake up in the middle of the night and see Santa Claus sitting in a chair in the corner of your room. Don't worry about it, he's just watching.
Fa-la-la-la-la-la

Jim Larsen

You better not cry
You better not cry
You better not cry
You better not cry
Crying will only make things worse.

He might try and crawl in bed with you.
He's not trying to be weird.
He just wants to cuddle
or maybe he wants to spoon.
If that makes you uncomfortable
just push him away.

"No" means no even when it's innocent. That's the true meaning of Christmas. It's what the Baby Jesus was born in the manger so, so long ago in the town of Bethlehem to remind us of, because there was no room in the inn. "No" means no. Please keep this in mind as you celebrate the holidays responsibly. Thank you.

Dying

I accept that I am a mortal being on the earth in this carnation for a limited amount of time, and sometimes I ponder what the means of my own demise will be. Then I tell myself it really doesn't matter how I die. All that matters is that the fans of the Darwin Awards get a good chuckle from it.

Jim Larsen

Stompy

Stomp, Stomp , Stompy.
Stompy stomp along.
An accident cost you all your toes,
now you walk all wrong.

Stompy stomp up the hill.
Stompy stomp downtown.
You got to keep momentum Stompy,
 or you will fall down.

Stompy is ten years old,
and he lost all his toes.
Now he can't play kickball.
That's just how it goes.

What happened, there was an accident.
It was with a saw.
But it wasn't Stompy's fault.
Blame it on his pa.

Now Stompy can't go on a hike.
He can barely ride his bike.
He can't jump
and he can't ski.
He can't even
climb a tree.

Stompy, stomp- Stompy stomp all night.
Stompy stomp all day.
Stomping's how you walk now, Stompy.
It's the only way.

Your father won't be home no more.
He's been put in jail.
It was for child endangerment,
your mom won't go his bail.

So stomp, stomp, Stompy.

Fat Naked Poetry

Make your mother proud.
Try to stomp quietly,
Stompy, you stomp too loud.

Toes give us balance, Stompy,
and you got none of that.
You got to keep moving Stompy,
or you will fall flat.

So stomp, Stompy stomp.
Stompy stomp along.
You can't take no gentle steps,
stomping's what you do.
So stomp, stomp, Stompy,
until your feet turn blue.

Stompy, Stomp down the street.
Then stomp on up the hill.
You will probably fall down though, Stompy,
if you are standing still.

So stomp, stomp Stompy.
Stompy stomp along.
People with all ten toes can walk with ease and grace.
But don't let stomping bother you, Stompy.
Keep a smile on your face.

You can still get around now, Stompy.
You just can't be in a hurry.
You'll never see your dad again.
He's been convicted by a jury.

Stompy is an inspiration now.
I think he is a hero.
Nothing ever bothers him
although his toes are zero.

So keep on stomping, Stompy.
Stompy keep on stomping.
Be stomp, stomp, stomping, Stompy.

Jim Larsen

Stompy, just stomp along.

Elevators

Sometimes I get on an elevator and I might see you coming, and you'll be calling, "Hold the door! Hold the door!" And I'll let the door get almost closed and then I'll hit the DOOR OPEN button. That way, you will know the door opened because of me, and now you owe me. Anything I want. Right down to your immortal soul. Not that I have any use for your pathetic little soul, but if you are offering it up for a free elevator ride, I'll take it. I'll take it and I'll put it in the jar with all the others. And if I want you to dance, I'll take my golden fiddle off the mantle, I'll rozzen up the bow, and you are going to dance for me, muthafucka! I'm telling you this because I reckon you ought to know what you are getting yourself into when you ride the elevators with me. You may thinks it's just a silly game that we are playing, and sure, maybe it is, but know this with absolute certainty: it's a game I intend to win.

Laughter

They say that laughter is the best medicine, but I know that is simply is not true. When my cousin was sick and was dying, we all took turns standing at his bedside laughing at him. "Ha ha ha!" We said. "You're dying!" It didn't make him feel any better. If anything, it only hastened his retreat from this planet.

Fire Queen

Ember on the arm
and smoke in the eyes,
The Fire Queen has arrived.

Fire!
Fire!
The Destroyer!
The Purger!
The Renewer!
The Sacred Spirit Flame!

All hail The Fire Queen!
She has arrived!
She has arrived!

Her name is Amy and she is from New Brunswick, which is a part of Canada up there where their police force are called "Mounties" and they ride horses across the frozen tundra, yodeling, and they always high-five each other when they make an arrest or give a speeding ticket or whatever. That's Canada for you. The people there are really cool, but it's a weird country.

Ember on the arm,
and smoke in the eyes.
The Fire Queen is here!

She lives in a cabana and Anne is her roommate. You know Anne, don't you? She's trying to quit smoking. She seems pretty cool, I guess.

Ember on the arm,
And smoke in the eyes.
The Fire Queen is here!

One time, she was driving the landscaping truck and she went speeding across the lawn and skidded to a stop in front of the tent where the managers were having a meeting, coming within an inch of one of the managers, and then she put the truck in neutral and revved it, and then just as she slammed it into gear, she yelled out the window to the managers, she yelled "Suck it bitches!" Then she sped away sending dirt and mud on the managers from the back tires of the truck. I was in the passenger seat when she was doing this, and I was like, "Oh my god, what is she doing?" Then I remembered, "Oh yeah. She's The Fire Queen. She can get away with shit like that."

Ember on the arm,
and smoke in the eyes.
The Fire Queen is here!
She's the volunteer of the week.

Ned's Bread

Ned baked bread for Ted, who said "Great bread, Ted. The he choked, his face turned red, and now he's dead. You're bread killed Ted, Ned.

Jim Larsen

Close Personal Friend of Jim Larsen

Jim Larsen is a writer, poet, philosophizer, and a humorist. He is the author of the widely popular books on tarot, What's Tarot Got To Do With It? The Fool's Path to Enlightenment and The Double Oh Fool Guide to Tarot Mastery. He has also written a four part series of meditations called Knowings from The Silence: Simple Wisdom for an Enlightened Life. He has a book of poetry called Fat Naked Poetry. Jim is also the writer/director of the 1998 cult classic film, Buttcrack.

Jim Larsen

Also by Jim Larsen

Knowings from The Silence: Simple Wisdom for an Enlightened Life

Knowings from The Silence: Simple Wisdom for an Enlightened Life Vol. 2

Knowings from The Silence: Simple Wisdom for an Enlightened Life Vol. 3

Knowings from The Silence: Simple Wisdom for an Enlightened Life Vol. 4

What's Tarot Got To With It? The Fool's Path to Enlightenment

The Double Oh Fool's Guide to Tarot Mastery

www.foolspathtarot.com
www.byjimlarsen.com

www.ingramcontent.com/pod-product-compliance
Lightning Source LLC
Chambersburg PA
CBHW071309040426
42444CB00009B/1942